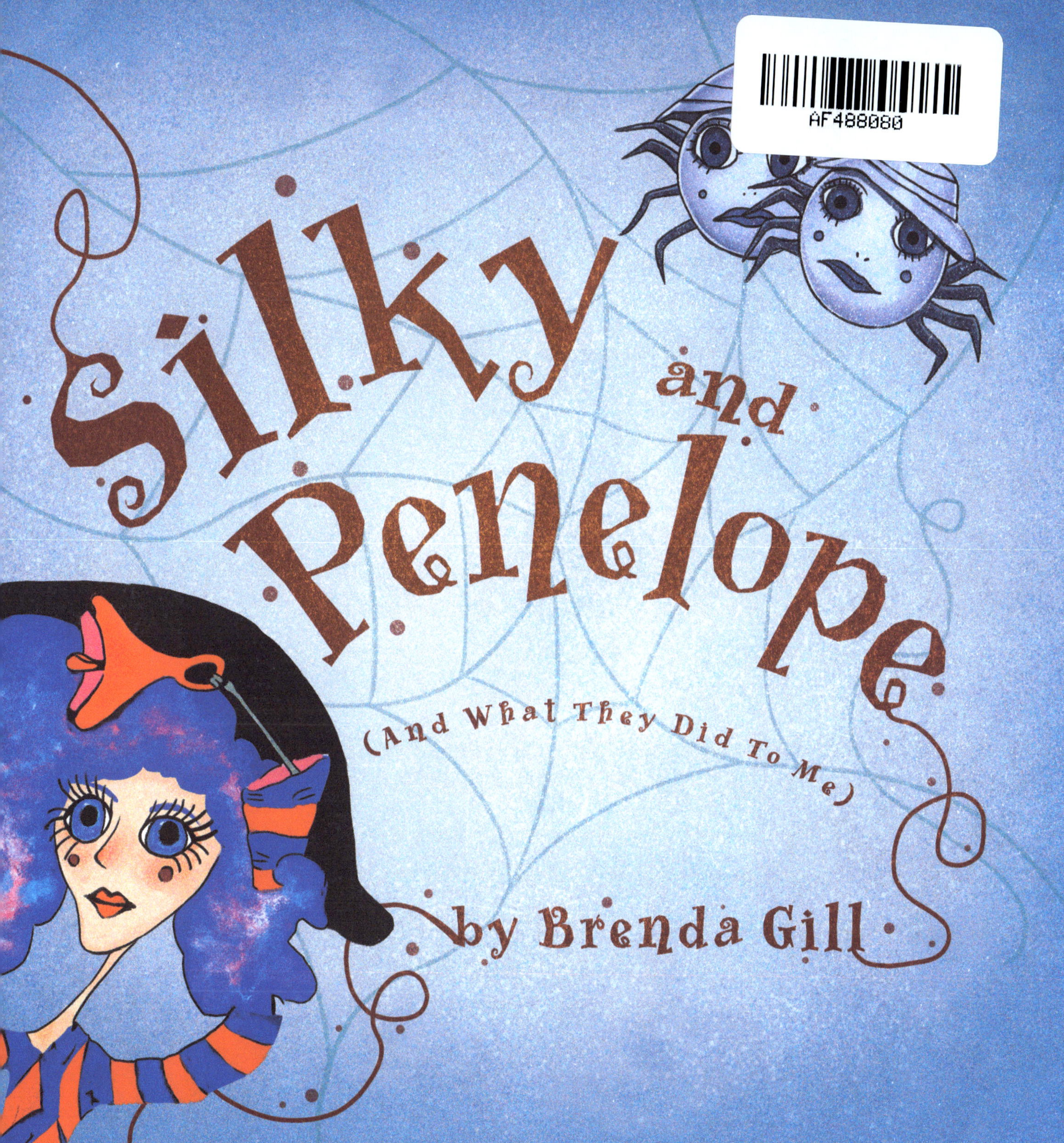

Silky
and
Penelope
(And What They Did To Me)
by Brenda Gill
AF488080

Silky and Penelope

(And What They Did To Me)

by Brenda Gill

Silky and Penelope
were spiders
in my Fairy Tree.
They were very
tricky,
and they
spun a web
for me.
They did not
like me
much at all,
for I was tall
and they were
very,
very,
small,
and they were scared
that with a touch
I'd brush them off,
and they would fall.
Oh no!
They did not like me
much at all!
They spun their web
so skillfully
I could not see it
in the light.
It vanished
from my sight.
And then they hid
behind a leaf.

It's my belief--
they giggled
while they
waited for
my fright.
I did not like the
spiders there,
living in my
Fairy Tree.
Now, the fairies--
they were
good to me.
Each night
by starlight
I would see
their dance,
their dreams
of fantasy,
all lit up
like a

Christmas tree--
they would dance,
and I could see.

I always thought,
when I went to bed,
that the dance was
just for me.
(although they
never said)

I'd see them
from my window,
as I was
lying there.
My head upon
my pillow,
I would turn each night

and stare.
One by one
they'd all light up,
and I could see
the fairies there,
making pretty patterns
as they danced
right in the air.
All the colors
of the rainbow showing,
I could see them
brightly glowing.
And they swirled,
and twirled,
and swung,
and whirled,
and sung
outside
my window.
Then at the end,
they'd form a line,
and take a bow,
and they were mine!

And I knew how
to cheer them on,
to make them sing
another song,
for I would ring
my fairy bell,
and that would tell
the fairies there,
that they could
do this
all night long.

Oh, how I miss
my fairy friends!
They don't come out

to dance for me,
since Silky
and Penelope
have moved
into my Fairy Tree.
Inside the tree
they hide from me
and even
lock their door!

I ring my bell
to try to tell
them,
"Come and play
some more.
Although I still
don't know
your names,
I love to see
your fairy games."

But all it did
was wake my dad,
and he was mad
for I was bad,
for playing toys
and making noise,
while he was
sleeping
in his bed.
He stuck his head
in through my door,
and it's a bore
but, this is what he said:

"You're in this room
to sleep my dear
and if another peep I
hear,
I'll get a broom

and sweep your toys
so far away,
no girls and boys
will want to come
into your empty
room to play!"
Then after that
I did not dare
to try to ring
my fairy bell.
Things were not
working very well,
while Silky and Penelope
were living in
my Fairy Tree.
"This has to end,"
said my Tree.
I thought that this
was just because
she was my

special friend,
and liked to see
me happy
when I headed
off to bed,
but now
she saw me weep
instead of
drifting deeply off
to sleep.
The visions of my fairies there,
all dancing in the starlight air
would keep away
the Nightmare fright
from scaring me awake at night.
The Nightmare was
a big bad horse
who flew on
shimmering shadowy beams

and tried to steal
my pleasant dreams:
of swings and songs
and sing-a-longs,
and happy days
and sunny plays
with wishing bones
and ice-cream cones.

My mother said,
"Now would you please
not eat that cheese
before you go to bed?
To me it seems
it brings bad dreams
And puts them in your head."
"It's not a dream, you see," I said.
"Cause twice before or maybe more,
the Nightmare came to me, in bed.
She was not only in my head,
but she was real,

for I could feel
her breathing,
hot upon my face.
She pressed on me with bended knee
and fought and caught me in my place.

But that was
long ago before
my fairy friends
moved in next door,
into my Fairy Tree.

And oh! I've been so happy,
when I've been sent to bed,
until now.
But anyhow,
that is not the
reason why

the Fairy Tree,
my friend,
has said,
"This spider thing
has got to end."
All night the fairies danced inside her;
to hide their magic from the spiders.
She simply could not sleep!

My Fairy Tree
waited many-a-day
for the Merry Winds
to come out and play,
and drive the spiders
from their keep.
And then one day
she got so mad,
(I think it was
from lack of sleep,)
but I was sad
when I heard her say,

"This has to end-
or I won't
be your friend!"
But the Merry Winds
had gone to sea,
and never came over
to play with me,
or with my crabby
Fairy Tree.
And Silky and Penelope
would hide from me
inside my Tree.
Then every time that
I came out
and tried to see
what this was
really all about,
I could hear them

laughing there,
And even though I'd
sit and stare,
I could not see them
hiding there.
My Fairy Tree
just would not talk
at all to me today
and so I turned
to walk away,
but not without
a backward shout
to Silky and Penelope
"I'll get you yet!"
And then, I think,
but I forget,
that's when I
stumbled
on a rock
and tumbled right
into their net!

Then everything
became a blur
of silken strands
that felt like hands
of elastic bands
and I was wrapped
from head to toe
with sticky stuff
that seemed like dough
but stuck so well like glue,
that if that wasn't
bad enough,
the smell was awful, too!

That Silky and Penelope!
I knew that
they were

watching me
and laughing
at me gleefully.
I just broke
down and cried.
I tried to hide
the trickling tears
that had begun
to slide.
I really tried
to give no place
to fears and tears
or jeers and cheers
but maybe,
just a little trace
of tears were
tickling my face.

To dream the dreams
of wishing wells
and magic spells

is not all that
it seems, I fear,
for I might be here
years and years
all tangled in this
spider's web,
dreaming dreams of
hopes and fears.
But just as I
began to wish
that I were
safely tucked away
inside my cozy bed,
a darkened shadow
flowed overhead.
The Nightmare showed
instead!
"You want to

ride with me?"
she said.
"I'll set you free
and we can
go away and play.
Then every night
and everyday,
we'll steal some
happy dreams away
and eat the
midnight hay."

"Oh no!" I said.
"I could not go
with you today.
It would not be
my sort of play,
to steal the happy
dreams away."

I thought it rather
brave of me
to speak to her
this way,
but the Nightmare
didn't notice
and she settled
down to stay.
Silky and Penelope
got such a dreadful scare
from the frightful sight
of that Nightmare
wanting to play
in such a nasty way
in the cold gray light
of that dismal day
that without a shout
or even a moan,
they looked at each other

and turned into stone!
And we were left
alone…

Just me and that
bad horse
were there,
And I was afraid
that she would force
me to fly away
with her somewhere.

It gave me such a
spooky scare,
for I was trapped
and hanging there,
wrapped and dangling,
right in the air,
stuck in the silky,
sticky web
all tangled
in the spider's lair.

I still heard
nothing
from my friend,
my Tree.
I thought it
was the end
for me!
I'm sorry to say,
it happened this way.
Because of my fears
I lost my cool
and shed a pool
of watery tears that day.

The Nightmare
rested by my Tree,

It seemed that she was
testing me.
She knew I did not
want to go.
I just kept shaking
my head no.
I just don't like
that kind of play
and surely don't eat
midnight hay!

I was shivering
and shaking.
All my bones
had started aching
and every part of me
was sore.
I knew that I
could not be taking
too much more of this

when suddenly
I heard a sound
(like a giant roar
and a splendid hiss)
the opening of
the Fairy door.

I think I flooded
out their floor,
for the fairies all
came dripping out,
all sopping wet
and hopping about.
But when they saw me
and my plight
they danced their
enchantment
to put things right,
splashing on the

Nightmare there,
and sprinkling sparkles in the air.

"Fairy dust and salty tears
make Nightmares disappear
for years."

The fairies sing
like bluebells ringing,
echoing on wings of song.
And when they dance
in daylight hour
their fairy power
is oh so strong!

The Nightmare then
looked a silly sight
as she flapped her wings
with all her might!

And by mistake
she chanced to take
the sticky spider's
web along.
As she pulled it
from the Tree
she quite by accident
set me free.

I fell right into
my pool of tears;
it seemed like
years ago I shed.
But I was laughing
now instead.
With joy I gazed
as the Nightmare raised
into the darkened sky
and as the Nightmare

passed me by,
I heard her give
a mournful cry,
"I won't be coming
back again,
for fairies give me
too much pain!"

Then suddenly
my mother came out
and she began to loudly shout,
"Your clothes are wet!
You get inside!"
Then all the fairies
ran to hide.

And to this day
I'll not forget
the sadness
and regret I feel.
I did not thank

the fairies then.
Though no one knows
my fairy friends,
they all are very real.

While still each night
I hear them sing
and watch them do their
fairy dance,
I never see them
play by day.
It was my only chance.

But very soon
one day at noon
the Merry Winds
blew from the sea
and dried my
teary pool for me.

My Fairy Tree
has once again
agreed to be
my special friend
and so you see
this is…

THE END

Silky and Penelope
(And What They Did To Me)©

Brenda Gill

9 798330 273089